Financial Reporting— a Management Briefing

Alan Warner

An MTP publication

First published in Great Britain October 1999 by

MTP Publishing,
3 Prebendal Court,
Oxford Road,
Aylesbury, HP19 3EY

ISBN 0 9536759 0 4

Typeset and printed by MFK Information Services Ltd,
23–25 Gunnels Wood Park,
Gunnels Wood Road,
Stevenage, Hertfordshire SG1 2BH

CONTENTS

AUTHOR'S ACKNOWLEDGEMENTS

I would like to thank colleagues at the Management Training Partnership for their assistance in producing this book. Firstly for their hard work in helping to release my time to write it, secondly for their support in developing content. The financial tutors at MTP continually share ideas and ways of explaining financial topics so that, at any time, the knowledge of one person is made up of the efforts and experience of the whole team.

I would particularly like to thank Kevin Amor, Alison Hennell and Mary Moore for their patience in responding to many and varied questions and for their detailed feedback on the content.

PREFACE

This book is about financial reporting, about the principles and concepts which underpin the production of financial statements, both internal and external. We strongly believe that it is essential for all managers to have this basic understanding, if they are to analyse and interpret financial information effectively.

The content is therefore unashamedly about accounting, because accounting is the set of tools with which financial reports are produced. And the pages that follow will show that these tools are frequently used to produce art rather than science. Accounting is an inexact process but an essential one for the management and control of any business.

The content of this book will be structured around the three key accounting statements – Profit & Loss Account, Cash Flow Statement, Balance Sheet – because they are central to all reporting, both internal and external. Knowing their purpose and their relationship to each other, is vital to understanding the financial dynamics of a business. Managing one of these three statements without the others is at best too narrow a focus and at worst can lead to business failure.

The style

Financial reporting can be complex and boring. That is why the most effective learning takes place when there is interaction and discussion, in particular when managers can see the impact of decisions on financial statements and ask appropriate questions.

In this book only the first chapter – an introduction and overview of the topic – is written in conventional form. Thereafter the style changes to interactive methods. Chapter two will demonstrate how a new company's financial position is monitored stage by stage through the reporting framework; it shows the impact of each decision and the relationship between the three accounting documents.

From Chapter 3 onwards we move to a different method of learning; the use of question and answer technique, the sort of questions that managers frequently ask and the answers which they should be given. This will hopefully make the text easier and more interesting to read, and also restrict content to those things which managers need to know. Financial reporting is a topic that can be extended almost without limit; we have deliberately aimed to keep this book focused on non-technical, management issues.

At times this means that we have deliberately avoided the complexity of real life accounting problems, because this can often get in the way of understanding fundamental principles. By avoiding technical complexity however, we are able to move onto some advanced issues of management applications which would not normally be included in a basic accounting book.

The book is for two main audiences; for managers who are to move on to more detailed study and who want to cover the more basic and generic concepts first. Also for those managers who want to check and improve their present understanding, maybe to assess whether more detailed study is required. The questions at the end of each chapter provide a good mechanism to make that judgement, as well as reinforcing learning; the answers are available as a separate document from MTP on request.

Its management focus is what makes this book different. It is not a text book, not an academic work, not a book which tries to cover all aspects of financial management. It is a practical management briefing about the key issues in financial reporting and we hope you find it helpful and enjoyable.

1

A framework
for financial
reporting

"I have the highest regard for accountants but they are generally not creative"

Sir Brian Wolfson

It has been the conventional wisdom in recent years that traditional 'financial' accounting is about bean counting and can be left to the accountants. Management accounting concepts like Activity Based Costing or Risk Analysis are the sort of topics which managers need to learn about in the modern business environment.

Though such topics are important, it can be argued that financial accounting is just as important to managers for a number of reasons:

Reason 1—Financial accounting provides the framework for all financial reporting

The main output of accounting is three documents which will be the framework for much of this book and its content. These three documents are:

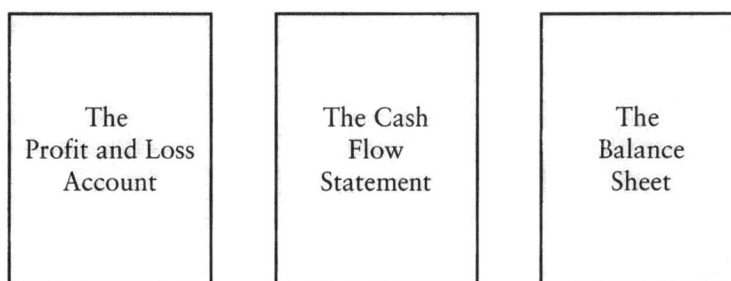

The Profit and Loss Account	The Cash Flow Statement	The Balance Sheet

They provide fundamental information about the business, its operating performance, its return to shareholders and its financial stability. Therefore financial accounts are of interest to analysts who study and compare businesses, to actual and potential investors and to bankers who lend them money.

Even more significant is the fact that almost every set of internal management accounts, however much they may be disguised with different terminologies and structures, are based upon these same three documents. Look at a retail operation and you will find that every store has its own "P & L". Cash flow statements are required for every division of multinational businesses as part of the regular reporting cycle. And

Balance Sheets, frequently adapted to company needs, are also required to assess the investment in each of these divisions and the return which is being made.

Reason 2—Financial results drive the share price

Though recent developments in Stock Markets have caused analysts to place less reliance on accounting documents than in the past, accounting information is still, in the short term, a major factor in the setting of share prices. The headline measure in press releases and analysts' reports is still Earnings per Share (profits after costs, tax and all other charges, divided by the number of ordinary shares issued) and this number is dependent upon a range of accounting practices and conventions which are to be described in this book.

Thus every manager should:

– Understand the impact of all business decisions on Earnings per Share (EPS), so as to be aware of the potential impact on the company's value to the outside world
– Sometimes be prepared to consider changing business decisions because of their potential impact on EPS
– Understand the accounting principles and conventions well enough to take part in informed debates with accounting specialists

Reason 3—Management can influence judgement areas which have an impact on financial results

There are a number of key areas where management judgement is fundamental to accounting results. The following are examples of questions which managers have to ask and answer before accounts can reflect the true business position.

How long will our assets last?	→	To fix depreciation periods
How much could we sell this old stock for?	→	To agree stock writedowns
How many of our customers will never pay?	→	To agree bad debt provisions
What is our liability for expenditure incurred but not invoiced?	→	To estimate the amount to be included in costs

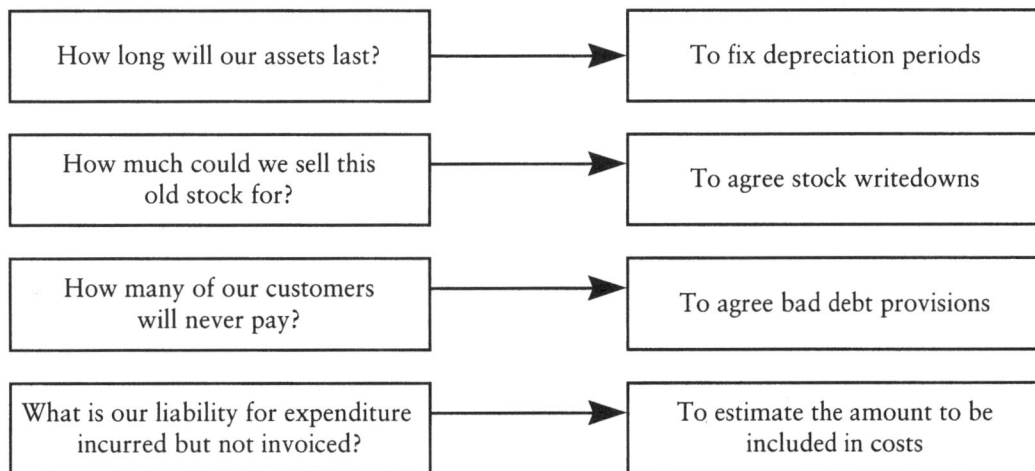

If these questions and answers are left to accounting people alone or are worked out on some mechanistic basis, the accounts may not reflect business reality. Managers have a role and a duty to take part in the debates about these issues and to make the figures as meaningful as possible to those who rely on them.

Fundamental Accounting concepts

These judgement areas can make those who study financial reports quite cynical about the validity of accounting information; there is the old joke about the accountant being asked to add up 2 + 2 and saying 'what would you like the answer to be? That is what 'creative accounting' is about—manipulating the methods to achieve a desired result.

For this reason there is a need for rules and regulation. There also has to be a series of underlying accounting concepts which provide the framework for checking that reasonable rather than 'creative' judgement has been applied. Later we will provide examples of these concepts when applied to specific accounting statements and situations. Here we will briefly lay out five fundamental principles which are 'generally accepted'.

PRINCIPLE ONE—PRUDENCE

Where accounting judgement is involved, it should veer on the side of prudence or conservatism. A profit should not be assumed until it is made; a loss should be assumed at an early stage. If in doubt the assumption which provides lower profit or lower asset values should be taken.

PRINCIPLE TWO—CONSISTENCY

Where a judgement has to be made it should be made consistently from one period to another. Thus the analyst who compares last year's results to this year should be comparing like with like. If there are occasions when accounting methods or policies have to be changed, the previous year's figures should also be changed and the impact of the new methods declared.

PRINCIPLE THREE—MATCHING

This principle refers predominantly to the Profit & Loss Account but, as will be seen in Chapter 2, the links between the three accounting statements mean that it is fundamental to all financial reporting. The matching principle means that the sales and the costs of running a business during a particular period must be matched together as closely as possible to arrive at a meaningful definition of profit. A knock-on effect of this 'Sales less Cost equals Profit' equation is that any expenditure which refers to future periods must be taken to the Balance Sheet as an asset.

PRINCIPLE FOUR—MATERIALITY

Financial statements must show all information which is necessary for their understanding; it is however permissible for information to be omitted if it is not material to the scale of the total figures. For example not every asset may need to be taken to the Balance Sheet; those that are small in the context of the company's scale of operations may be 'written off' as costs in the year in which they are spent.

PRINCIPLE FIVE—GOING CONCERN

This principle says that, unless there is information to the contrary, the business is assumed to be a going concern and to continue in its present form. This principle is particularly relevant to asset valuation and its implications will be discussed in Chapter 4.

The production of good accounting information therefore requires the application of these principles within the context of each unique business; it also requires the development of specific accounting policies to cover particular issues and situations. This often requires judgement about which of the above five principles should take priority where there is a potential conflict.

It is not therefore surprising that shareholders and others who use published financial information like to see a statement of the accounting policies used by each company and confirmation that 'generally accepted accounting principles'—GAAP—have been applied. The independence of the auditors who provide external verification is therefore vital to the credibility of published financial information.

The Users of Financial Reports

As companies became bigger, more complex and publicly quoted, legal and regulatory frameworks have developed. Accounts have become more available to public scrutiny and a range of users, all with different objectives, have evolved. There are now three main categories of user who have distinctly different areas of focus:

```
                    ┌─────────────────────┐
                    │  Users of Financial │
                    │      Accounts       │
                    └─────────────────────┘
            ┌──────────────┼──────────────┐
   ┌────────────────┐ ┌──────────────┐ ┌──────────────┐
   │   Management   │ │  Shareholder │ │    Banker    │
   │   Perspective  │ │  Perspective │ │  Perspective │
   └────────────────┘ └──────────────┘ └──────────────┘
           │                 │                │
   ┌────────────────┐ ┌──────────────┐ ┌──────────────┐
   │   Operational  │ │  Shareholder │ │   Stability  │
   │   Performance  │ │    Return    │ │  and Survival│
   └────────────────┘ └──────────────┘ └──────────────┘
```

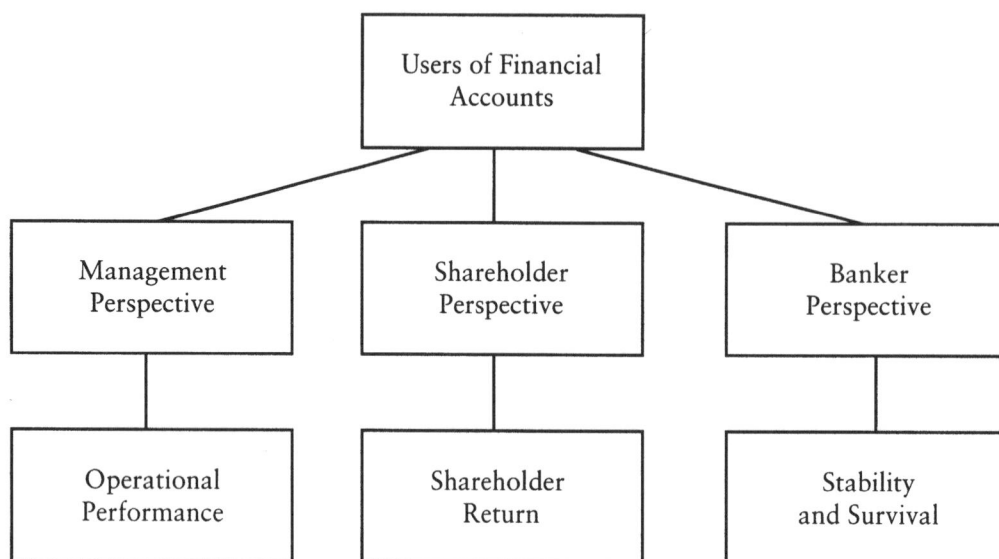

The study of accounts from a management perspective is not confined to the managers of the company. This applies to anyone who analyses financial information in order to judge how well the business is managed at the operating level; for instance it could include suppliers, competitors and customers.

The emphasis of this kind of analysis is likely to be on the sales made and on the costs of running the business, down to Operating Profit level ; also on those items in the Balance Sheet which reflect operating performance, particularly the investment in fixed assets and the levels of stock and debtors. Issues like tax and debt structure would not come within the scope of this perspective.

The shareholder perspective would, in contrast, require analysis of the full structure of the Profit & Loss Account, right down to the final profit attributable to shareholders and the dividends paid. This is the correct perspective of both actual and potential shareholders for whom operational performance is only part of the story. They look at the Profit & Loss Account to show what they are getting out of the business and at the Balance Sheet to see what they have already put in.

The third and final perspective is fundamentally different. In addition to bankers this perspective would also be taken by credit agencies and suppliers who are assessing credit worthiness. Their focus is more on whether the business will survive and less on whether it is performing well. Bankers examine the Balance Sheet more than the Profit & Loss Account and their main focus is the loans outstanding and the assets which are available to repay them if things go wrong. It is true that they also examine the Profit & Loss Account and the Cash Flow but the emphasis is more on ability to service debt than on management performance or shareholder return.

With the background of such diverse perspectives, it is perhaps not surprising that there are frequent expressions of dissatisfaction with the information in financial accounts. How could one set of information meet such diverse needs to the complete satisfaction of all?

Reinforcement Questions

(1)   What is the most common 'headline' measure which drives share prices and which comes from a set of accounts?

(2)   Is this measure before or after tax?

(3)   Which of the three accounting documents does this measure come from?

(4)   Would the use of the prudence concept cause provisions for bad debts to be higher or lower?

(5)   Which of the five accounting concepts is likely to be most useful when comparing the long term trends from a set of accounts?

(6)   What are the three perspectives taken by analysts of financial reports?

(7)   Which level of profit is likely to be taken by analysts who adopt the 'management' perspective when analysing financial reports?

(8)   Who else might take this perspective, apart from the management themselves?

(9)   Which level of profit is likely to be taken by analysts who adopt the shareholder perspective when analysing financial reports?

(10)   Which of the three accounting documents has traditionally been the main focus of analysis by bankers?

The answers to these reinforcement questions and those for other chapters will be provided on request to:

Management Training Partnership plc
3 Prebendal Court
Oxford Road
Aylesbury
Bucks
HP19 3EY

Telephone   (0)1296 423474
E-mail   mtp_office@compuserve.com

Where this book is given as pre-work for an MTP course the answers will be provided by the tutor.

2

The relationship between the accounting documents

"I don't believe money is no object. Money is the object"

James Gulliver

We can now begin to examine the linkage between the three accounting documents and, at the same time, answer some important questions which lie at the heart of financial measurement, for example:

- How does the Balance Sheet maintain its balance and what does this mean?
- Does every financial transaction have an impact on all three documents?
- What is the relationship between the Cash Flow Statement and the cash figure in the Balance Sheet?
- What is the relationship between the Profit & Loss Account and Retained Profits in the Balance Sheet?

The best way of demonstrating the impact of decisions on the accounting documents is by looking at single transactions, one by one. To show this impact we will introduce a Balance Sheet structure which provides the best framework to show the linkages between the documents. There are different Balance Sheet structures which will be discussed further in Chapter 4 but the framework we will use at this stage is:

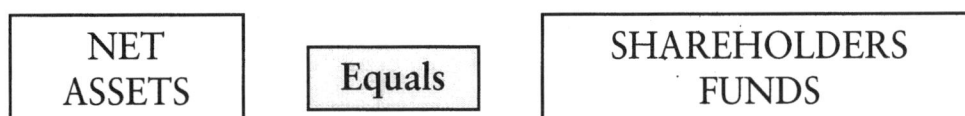

NET ASSETS	Equals	SHAREHOLDERS FUNDS

With this structure the Balance Sheet is showing, on one side, how much money has been put in by shareholders and, on the other side, the assets which have been bought with their money; the continuing balance shows that every penny has been accounted for. That is the fundamental purpose of a Balance Sheet.

If we also consider that:

- One of the assets in "Net Assets" is cash in hand, the result of what has happened to cash flow so far and....
- One of the entries in Shareholders Funds is Retained Profits, the result of what has happened to the Profit & Loss Account so far...

then it is possible to see the Balance Sheet as the framework for all three documents. The following diagram shows the link in visual form:

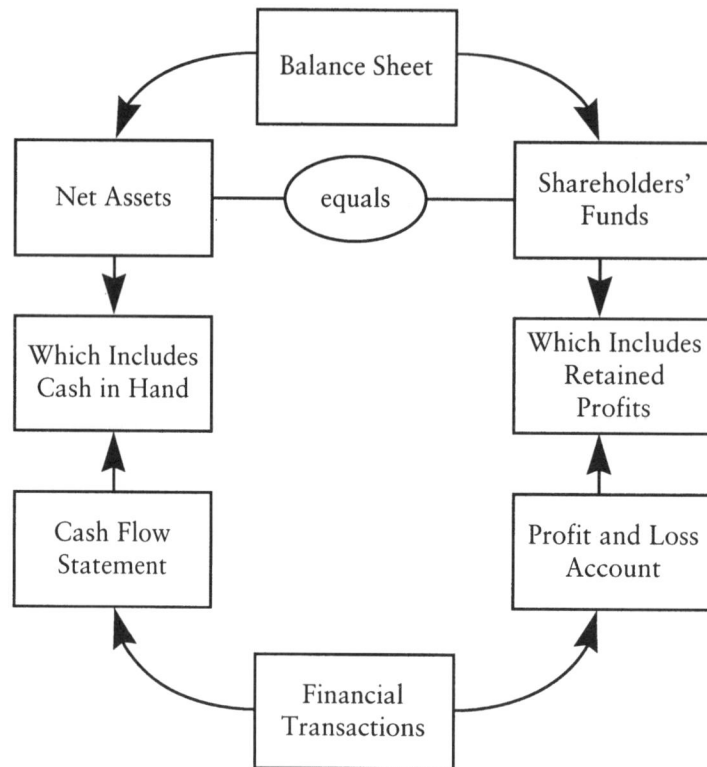

```
                          ┌──────────────┐
                          │ Balance Sheet│
                          └──────────────┘
          ┌─────────────┐   ┌───────┐   ┌──────────────┐
          │  Net Assets │───│ equals│───│ Shareholders'│
          │             │   └───────┘   │    Funds     │
          └─────────────┘               └──────────────┘
                 │                              │
          ┌─────────────┐               ┌──────────────┐
          │Which Includes│              │Which Includes│
          │Cash in Hand  │              │  Retained    │
          │              │              │   Profits    │
          └─────────────┘               └──────────────┘
                 ▲                              ▲
          ┌─────────────┐               ┌──────────────┐
          │  Cash Flow  │               │Profit and Loss│
          │  Statement  │               │   Account     │
          └─────────────┘               └──────────────┘
                 ▲           ┌──────────┐        ▲
                 └───────────│ Financial│────────┘
                             │Transactions│
                             └──────────┘
```

In order to illustrate this further we will go back to the birth of a company. We will have to simplify to help the learning process. An important simplification we are making is that financial transactions happen and are recorded one by one. In reality of course this is not the case—many financial transactions take place over an accounting period and are summarised at the time the accounts are prepared.

When a company first starts, someone has to put in money which is recorded as Share Capital. We will assume that John Risktaker (JR) has gone into business and has raised £10,000 Share Capital from himself and from family and friends; the company issues shares to them in recognition of their investment. As Shareholders they are entitled to share future profits and dividends with him in proportion to their investment.

Transaction 1

JR collects the money from his new shareholders and pays it into a new bank account which he opens in the company's name.

The impact on the Balance Sheet is as follows:

NET ASSETS		= SHAREHOLDERS FUNDS	
Cash	£10,000	Share Capital	£10,000
	£10,000		£10,000

This simple transaction confirms the previously stated role of the Balance Sheet—to show the Shareholders what they have put in and what the management has done with their money. At this stage the Balance Sheet shows that it is still being held in cash. Soon they will see what John does with it and this will help them to judge how well he is running the business.

Note that at this stage there has been no impact on the P & L (which will eventually appear in Shareholders Funds) because the company has not yet started to trade. There has been an impact on Cash Flow—the £10,000 has come into the bank account to create the £10,000 balance.

Transaction 2

JR buys a van to deliver goods for £3,000 cash.

The Balance Sheet—note that we will always be showing its CUMULATIVE position—now looks like this.

NET ASSETS		= SHAREHOLDERS FUNDS	
Vehicle	£3,000		
Cash	£7,000	Share Capital	£10,000
	£10,000		£10,000

This transaction involves the exchange of one asset for another; cash has been taken out of the bank account by the drawing of a cheque and, in its place, there is now a vehicle. This is an asset, something which will provide future benefit to the business.

This transaction again has no impact on the P & L because there has been no trading activity. Another way of confirming that there is no impact on the P & L is to say that assets are, in total, exactly the same as before; thus no profit or loss has been made and no entry in the P & L is necessary.

Note that there is an impact on Cash Flow—there is a negative change of £3,000 bringing the balance down to £7,000. The Cash Flow Statement can thus be seen as a window within the Net Assets section of the Balance Sheet. The £7,000 balance is shown and this is the outcome of a Cash Flow Statement which contains a series of transactions (so far zero starting point plus £10,000 minus £3,000).

Note also that the Vehicle is shown before Cash. Although layout and sequence do not have any impact on the total or its ability to balance, there are particular conventions. We are following the European convention which says that the more permanent assets come first. In the USA the convention is completely the reverse; the list of assets starts with the most liquid and realisable, so Cash would come before Vehicles.

The present Balance Sheet valuation of this asset is at its cost of £3,000. At a later stage we will need to address the issue of depreciation—how far we need to reduce that initial value at the end of the accounting period.

Transaction 3

JR now buys some stock of the goods in which he is to trade, for £4,500, paid for in cash

NET ASSETS		= SHAREHOLDERS FUNDS	
Vehicle	£3,000		
Stock	£4,500		
Cash	£2,500	Share Capital	£10,000
	£10,000		£10,000

Again this is just an exchange of one asset for another so there is no impact on the P & L. It is only when the stock is sold and included as "Cost of Sales" that there is an impact on P & L. There is an impact on Cash Flow which moves the cash balance down by £4,500 to £2,500 as the cash is paid.

Note that Stock appears between Vehicle and Cash as it is less permanent than the Vehicle but more permanent (and less realisable) than Cash.

Transaction 4

He recruits an administrator and pays wages of £500.

This transaction is different because we are not buying another asset as we did in the case of the vehicle and stock. We are spending money on a service which we need today to run the business, we are incurring cost or "Revenue Expenditure". This cannot be shown as an asset so we need to open a Profit & Loss Account to record the transaction. We must also record the fact that we have reduced cash but have not replaced it with anything else that we can call an asset.

The impact of this transaction is as follows:

NET ASSETS			= SHAREHOLDERS FUNDS		
Vehicle	£3,000		Share Capital	£10,000	
Stock	£4,500				
Cash	£2,000		Profit & Loss	(500)	
	£9,500			£9,500	

The negative Profit and Loss Account balance of £500 arises because at this stage a cost has been incurred and there have been no sales; thus the result of the "Sales less Cost" equation is a loss of £500. The Balance Sheet is recording the fact that, at this early stage, some of the Shareholders' initial investment has been lost.

This transaction confirms an important principle of financial measurement through the framework of the three documents. It explains why the Balance Sheet balances and how the linkages take place. This principle is:

A loss through the P & L arises when there is a loss of Net Asset value compared to the previous Balance Sheet position.

and

A profit through the P & L arises where there is a gain in Net Asset value, in fact that is one way of defining profit.

This important principle becomes even more apparent from the next transaction.

Transaction 5

Half of the stock is sold for £3,000 cash.

A profit of £750 has now been made—goods which cost £2,250 (half of £4,500) have been sold for £3,000. The Balance Sheet now looks like this:

NET ASSETS		= SHAREHOLDERS FUNDS	
Vehicle	£3,000	Share Capital	£10,000
Stock	£2,250		
Cash	£5,000	Profit & Loss A/C	250
	£10,250		£10,250

The assets side is showing £750 more Net Assets than before because of this profitable transaction. The Shareholders Funds side confirms that this profit has been made and records it as part of the Shareholders' investment in the business.

At this point the cumulative profit position, as shown through the Profit & Loss Account, is as follows:

Sales	3,000
Cost of Sales	(2,250)
Expenses	(500)
Profit	250

This confirms what was stated earlier—that the Shareholders Funds side of the Balance Sheet contains the bottom line of the P & L Account. At this stage it is appearing as "Profit & Loss A/c" and sometimes that heading is used. A more descriptive and commonly used term as the business expands is "Retained Profit"; at this point a profit of £250 has been made and has not yet been distributed to Shareholders.

Transaction 6

The other half of the stock is sold for £2,750, this time on credit.

For the first time we have a transaction which does not involve cash. Nevertheless a profit has, in accounting terms, still been made and this will have an impact on the Balance Sheet. The Balance Sheet now changes as follows:

NET ASSETS		= SHAREHOLDERS FUNDS	
Vehicle	£3,000	Share Capital	£10,000
Stock	—		
Debtors	£2,750		
Cash	£5,000	Profit & Loss A/C	750
	£10,750		£10,750

Net Assets have increased by £500 because we have sold goods which cost £2,250 for £2,750. A new asset has been created in the form of a debtor (called "Accounts Receivable" in the USA) which represents a promise of money from the customer. The Profit & Loss Account shows this £500 profit as part of Shareholders' Funds and thus causes the cumulative "Retained Profit" to rise from £250 to £750.

In recording this £500 as a profit we are making an important assumption—that the £2,750 will eventually be received and that the Balance Sheet valuation is therefore valid. If there is any doubt about this a view has to be taken—one of the management judgement areas we discussed in Chapter One.

If for instance it was later discovered that a dispute about pricing was likely to cause only £2,650 to be received, the debtor should then be reduced (what accountants call being 'written down') to this amount and £100 lower profit would be recorded.

Transaction 7

Further stock to the value of £1,000 is bought, this time on credit.

Again we have a business transaction which does not involve cash flow—note that the cash balance remained on £5,000 throughout transaction 6 and this will happen again.

The impact of this transaction is different from what has gone before because for the first time we are showing a negative number on the assets side, which explains why we have so far referred to that side as NET Assets. The Balance Sheet now looks like this:

NET ASSETS		= SHAREHOLDERS FUNDS	
Vehicle	£3,000	Share Capital	£10,000
Stock	£1,000		
Debtors	£2,750		
Cash	£5,000	Profit & Loss A/C	750
Creditors	(£1,000)		
	£10,750		£10,750

This reduction of creditors would normally be shown after a sub-total. A line would be drawn under cash to show Total Assets of £11,750, then there would be a reduction of £1,000 to arrive at the Net Assets total. This has a certain logic which could be applied to our everyday lives; we might add up a total of all the assets we own but, to get a true idea of our wealth, we need to take off our liabilities to arrive at the net position.

This treatment of creditors and other external liabilities is the main distinction between this layout and the more traditional "Assets equals Liabilities" structure which is still used in many countries. In that case the balancing principle would still apply. Creditors would be added to Shareholders Funds to arrive at £11,750 Total Liabilities and this would balance with Total Assets.

Transaction 8

Other administrative expenses of £200 are paid in cash.

NET ASSETS		= SHAREHOLDERS FUNDS	
Vehicle	£3,000	Share Capital	£10,000
Stock	£1,000		
Debtors	£2,750		
Cash	£4,800	Profit & Loss A/C	550
Creditors	(£1,000)		
	£10,550		£10,550

Again we have an item of cost which will appear in the P & L to reduce the profit balance from £750 to £550

Transaction 9

It is the end of the first month and it is decided to take 2% depreciation on the vehicle (equivalent to 24% pa).

We will discuss depreciation in more detail in later chapters but this is a first opportunity to see its double impact. The 2% is applied to the vehicle's original cost of £3000 to arrive at £60. This accounting entry reduces the value of the asset in the Balance Sheet and simultaneously becomes a cost in the P & L, thus reducing the profit by £60.

NET ASSETS		= SHAREHOLDERS FUNDS	
Vehicle	£2,940	Share Capital	£10,000
Stock	£1,000		
Debtors	£2,750		
Cash	£4,800	Profit & Loss A/C	490
Creditors	(£1,000)		
	£10,490		£10,490

Note that once again the cash position has not changed; the impact on cash came when the asset was originally purchased.

Transaction 10

JR takes out a loan of £2000 from a finance company to support future investment and the money is paid into his bank. No interest is chargeable for the first month.

Under this Balance Sheet layout, loans are treated in the same way as creditors; as a reduction in the 'Net assets' section. The Balance Sheet would look like this:

NET ASSETS		= SHAREHOLDERS FUNDS	
Vehicle	£2,940	Share Capital	£10,000
Stock	£1,000		
Debtors	£2,750		
Cash	£6,800	Profit & Loss A/C	490
Creditors	(£1,000)		
Loan	(£2,000)		
	£10,490		£10,490

Cash has increased because the new loan has been paid into the bank account but there is a compensating reduction within Net Assets by the same amount; thus the total remains the same. As there is not yet any interest cost, there is no impact on the P & L Account.

An important piece of information is now available from the Balance Sheet—the proportion of loan finance (Debt) to shareholder investment (Equity). This is known as *gearing or leverage* and is of particular interest to those who take the 'bankers' perspective of analysis.

The Closing Balance Sheet

We now have a complete Balance Sheet at the end of the period. The above structure is more or less what appears in published accounts throughout the world. As we will see in Chapter 4, there are a number of subtotals, in particular the 'Fixed Assets'—for example the vehicle—will be separated from the 'Current Assets'—Stock, Debtors and Cash.

Reconciling the Cash Flow Statement and Profit & Loss Account

This Balance Sheet has an entry for Cash of £6,800 within Net Assets and for Profit & Loss A/c of £490 within Shareholders Funds. The key to why the Balance Sheet balances and to how it provides control of the business, is the fact that these balances are the accumulated totals of the other two documents—the Cash Flow Statement and the Profit & Loss Account.

We can now prove this by showing simplified versions of these two statements which confirm that they arrive at these final balances.

Cash Flow Statement	£
Opening Cash	0
Cash in:	
New Share Capital	10,000
Cash sales	3,000
New loan	2,000
Total Cash in	15,000
Cash out:	
Vehicle purchase	(3,000)
Stock purchased for cash	(4,500)
Administrator's wages	(500)
Administrative expenses	(200)
Total Cash out	(8,200)
Closing cash	£6,800

Profit and Loss Account	£
Sales (both cash and credit)	5,750
Cost of sales (all stock consumed)	(4,500)
Administrator's wages	(500)
Administrative expenses	(200)
Depreciation	(60)
Total costs	(5,260)
Profit	490

In the next Chapter we will explore the Profit & Loss Account further and show how costs can be categorised and how the various levels of profit—Gross Profit, Operating Profit, Profit after tax—are calculated. In Chapters 4 and 5 we will go into more depth about the Balance Sheet and Cash Flow Statement and the various structures which have evolved. This worked example provides the essential understanding of the linkages between the three documents which is necessary to move to this next stage.

Reinforcement Questions and Exercise

(1)   Which type of asset would you expect to see first in the Balance Sheet layout described in this chapter?

(2)   How might this be different in the USA?

(3)   What impact does the purchase of stock have on the Profit & Loss Account?

(4)   What impact does a credit sale have on the Profit & Loss Account?

(5)   Does every accounting transaction have an impact on both sides of the Balance Sheet?

(6)   What impact does depreciation have on cash flow?

(7)   Will 'Share Capital' always stay at the same number (£10,000), throughout the life of the company?

(8)   What would be the impact on the Balance Sheet if the bank charged 1% interest on the loan?

(9)   What would be the impact on the Balance Sheet if the creditor was paid in cash?

(10) Produce an answer in similar 'stage by stage' form to the example in this chapter, recording the following transactions for the first month of a company's life:

(a)   Share Capital of £50,000 raised and paid in
(b)   First month's rent on premises paid in cash—£5,000
(c)   Equipment bought for use in the business—£15000 cash
(d)   Stock purchased on credit—£20,000
(e)   Wages paid to staff—£3,000 cash
(f)   Sales made on credit—£27,000, all stock sold
(g)   Creditor of £20,000 is paid
(h)   Credit customer pays the whole amount owing
(i)   Equipment depreciated at 1% per month

3

The Profit & Loss Account

"If you're not in business for fun or profit, what the hell are you doing here?"

Robert Townsend

What does a P & L really tell you about a business?

The specific purpose of the P & L Account is to measure management performance; it compares the sales of a particular period with the costs of running the business during that same period. The excess of sales over costs, the profit, represents increased wealth for the business and is recognised as a good measure of management success.

Why is a P & L necessary?

Because the financial information which comes naturally out of a business, the cash position from the bank statement, does not provide a good measure of management performance in the short term. For instance, you may be performing well but have a negative cash flow in a particular year because of cash invested for the future.

How is a P & L structured?

At a detailed level there are many variations in structure. The underlying equation is "SALES less COSTS equals PROFIT" and the variations and complexity should not be allowed to hide that fundamental MATCHING process. MATCHING is one of the fundamental concepts of accounting which was referred to in Chapter One. We try to match a period's sales with the costs incurred in making those sales and only if sales and costs are truly matched can a valid profit for the period be produced.

Over what period is it taken?

The year is the basic period for external reporting though internally it may be monthly or even weekly. More recently it has become normal for Stock Exchanges to require quoted companies to report to shareholders half yearly and even quarterly.

What do we mean by sales?

We mean the amounts charged for goods delivered or services provided to customers during that period, not the orders placed, not the cash collected, just the amounts charged.

How are sales categorised?

Though each company will have its own ways of dividing sales—for instance by product or by region—the normal presentation of a Profit & Loss Account does not provide any split. Sales are normally shown as one number alone, excluding VAT or other sales taxes.

What do we mean by costs?

We mean the cost of resources consumed during that same period, so that there is a true match with the sales figure. For example, it would not be the amount paid in cash for rent or electricity which goes in the P & L, but the cost of the amount used.

How are costs categorised?

Internally companies will have many different ways of classifying costs, depending on the nature of the business.

The minimum breakdown in most businesses and most published accounts is between:

Cost of Sales

and

Operating Expenses

Then, lower down the Profit & Loss Account, there is a further breakdown of items which are appropriations of profit rather than operating costs, ie:

- **Interest costs**
- **Tax**
- **Dividends to shareholders**

So how would a Profit & Loss Account normally look with this categorisation?

A simplified structure, using only the above cost categories and with no complex features, would look like this:

Sales	1,000
Cost of Sales	(550)
Gross Profit	450
Operating Expenses	(350)
Operating Profit	100
Interest Costs	(25)
Profit before Tax	75
Tax	(35)
Profit after Tax (Earnings)	40
Dividends	(20)
Retained Profit	20

Note

Interest costs are amounts charged to the company for short or long term loans; dividends are cash distributions of profit to shareholders.

Why does it have to be complicated with all these subtotals?

This is so that performance can be analysed at various levels of profitability. For instance the first level—Gross Profit—is the profit after the Cost of Sales, the actual cost of making the products in a manufacturing business. This helps anyone studying the accounts to know how much profit is being made at that level and to make comparisons with previous periods and with other companies.

Aren't there normally much more comprehensive analyses of costs than the one above?

There are almost as many ways of analysing costs as there are companies. Internally it depends on the needs of management and how they like to manage and control costs. Externally companies are reluctant to disclose more than they are required to do by regulation, because competitors will find out about their cost structure.

Cost of Sales and Operating Expenses would typically be broken down like this:

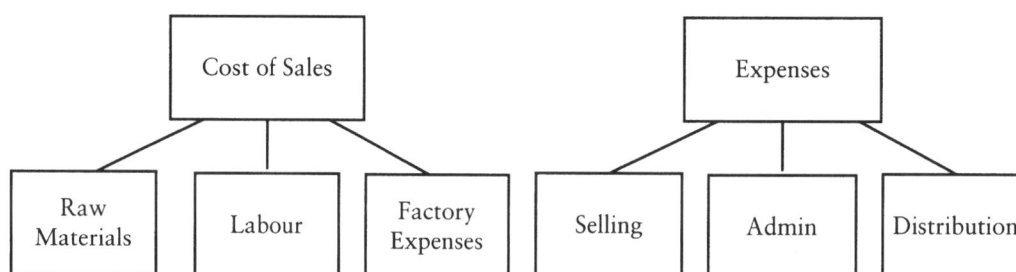

This seems relevant to a manufacturing business but what about non-manufacturing? Do they have similar cost splits and do they arrive at Gross Profit and Operating Profit?

Operating Profit is worked out by more or less every business. However to arrive at Gross Profit, you need a meaningful definition of Cost of Sales. This is easy for some businesses like retailing where the Cost of Sales would be the merchandise and Gross Profit would be the profit at the shop counter. With other non-manufacturing businesses—say an airline or a telecommunications company—Gross Profit is a less relevant concept and, if worked out internally, would be dependent on each company's own categories and definitions. There is very little standardisation in cost definition between companies so it can be misleading to make comparisons.

Does this mean that it is impossible to compare the Gross Profit of one company with another?

It means that it is very difficult and has to be undertaken with care. There are examples of companies which appear to change normal definitions when publishing results to the outside world. For example while most retailers use the definition of Gross Profit mentioned above, some others change that definition to "profit after all store costs" when complying with the UK accounting requirement to disclose a Gross Profit number. There are some suspicions that they may do this to avoid disclosing their true gross profits to competitors.

What about the validity of comparing lower levels of profit in the P & L, for example Operating Profit, Profit before and after Tax, Earnings, Retained Profit?

Generally the lower you go down the P & L, the more valid the comparison, because the split of costs becomes less important. For example, Operating Profit is after all operating costs and, however you classify them between Cost of Sales and Operating Expenses, the profit number will be the same.

So it will always be valid to compare two Operating Profit numbers?

It depends what you are trying to do. Because of the 'Consistency' concept mentioned in Chapter One, it should be valid to compare the Operating Profit number of a company with its results from the previous period, to see how much it has improved, both in money terms and as a percentage of sales. If you are trying to compare the Operating Profit of one company with another, that will be much more difficult because there may be different accounting policies and different operational conditions. So you should only do so with awareness of these problems.

In published accounts, who would look at the various profit levels and why?

To answer this question properly, you have to remember the three different perspectives of analysis from Chapter One:

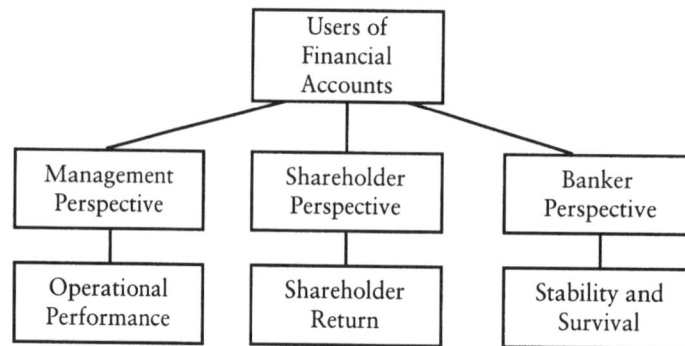

Management perspective

The managers and business analysts taking this perspective would look at the *Gross Profit* and *Operating Profit* lines and any cost analysis which is available. They would compare the profits with the previous year and with the performance of competitors, working out percentages of sales or capital invested.

Shareholder perspective

The Shareholders and Stock Exchange analysts taking this perspective would look at the *Earnings* line, the after tax profit left for shareholders, and the *Dividends* to be distributed. They would calculate the growth of these two numbers compared to the previous year and assess whether, in their view, the right level of profit is being made and whether the distribution policy is reasonable.

Banker perspective

The bankers, credit agencies and suppliers who take this perspective are more interested in the company's ability to service debt so they will focus on the *Profit before Interest* and its relationship to the *Interest*

Costs. They will be particularly concerned to see how much of the profit is absorbed by interest as this is a key indicator of a company's ability to survive.

In every case analysts are likely to compare with the previous year and with norms for the sector and the business environment. This emphasis on the key areas of interest in the P & L is not to the exclusion of other lines or items, it is merely the main focus and starting point. For example, the Shareholder who is looking for reasons why Earnings and Dividend have declined might then move into analysis of changes to interest costs and other levels of profit.

To what extent does the P & L Account require judgement to arrive at the numbers?

The matching concept constantly requires judgement to be used; matching sales against costs is actually quite difficult. For example, when calculating energy costs it is often difficult to calculate precisely how much electricity has been used in one year and how much in another. Estimates of usage may have to be made, particularly if the bill has not yet been received – this is what is called an ACCRUAL.

It may also be difficult to judge the extent to which a major programme of long term repairs and improvements should be shown as costs in the year in which the work takes place, or how far it should be treated as Capital Expenditure and spread over several years through depreciation.

Do the judgements only apply to costs or can sales also be difficult to calculate?

It depends on the business. In most cases it is relatively easy to arrive at a sales number but there are some industries where judgements apply to both sales and costs. For instance, how do you apportion the sales and costs of a civil engineering or shipbuilding project which may last several years? Estimates have to be made and accounting conventions agreed so that there is no danger of profits being deliberately over or under stated. Analysts who specialise in businesses of this kind have to know the methods and the issues involved so that they can check on the conventions and assess their validity.

How does depreciation fit into the P & L format we've examined so far?

Depreciation is one of the costs in the P & L Account but is not normally shown separately in the main body of the document. It will always be possible to find a total depreciation number in notes to externally published accounts but its component parts will usually reside separately within the various functional headings. In a manufacturing business the depreciation on factory equipment will be contained within "Cost of Sales" and depreciation on other equipment (for example on office machines) within "Expenses".

Does this mean that depreciation is just like any other cost?

In one sense it does; it reminds managers that depreciation is part of the cost headings for which they are responsible. But, although depreciation is contained within other headings, it is fundamentally different from most other costs in that it is a BOOK ENTRY. It shows the impact of past capital investment and charges an appropriate amount to the accounting period. It does not involve any outlay of cash.

Why is it so important to remember this?

Because it is fundamental to the way cash flow statements are reported, as we will see in Chapter 5. For example, if we look again at the numbers in the earlier P & L structure:

Sales	1,000
Cost of Sales	(550)
Gross Profit	450

Let's assume that this company had bought factory equipment in that year for (say) £500 and its estimated life was 10 years, so the depreciation would be £50. It would appear in the Profit & Loss Account within Cost of Sales and would be part of the £550.

Assuming that this £50 is the only depreciation and that all other costs do involve cash outlay, the CASH spending on Cost of Sales in that year would only be £500, the total of £550 less the book entry of £50 depreciation. This means that, assuming Sales are also for cash, the Gross Profit in CASH terms would be £50 more than the £450 previously shown, ie:

Sales	1,000
Cost of Sales – cash outlays	(500)
Gross Profit in cash terms	500

Another way to arrive at this number is to add back the depreciation of 50 to the gross profit of 450, an approach which is used in some cash flow statements described in Chapter 5.

Do the longer term costs like research or advertising get included in the P & L Account, just like any other costs?

Yes, they normally do. The alternative would be to take them to the Balance Sheet as an asset, reflecting their future value to the business. However this is generally felt to be against the PRUDENCE concept which underpins much accounting thinking.

But doesn't this mean that the profits of one year could be misleading because of exceptionally high or low spending in these areas?

Yes. This accounting convention means that profits will fall if there is an exceptional investment in these areas in one particular year. And conversely that a company can manipulate profits in the short term by cutting back on these and other discretionary costs. Thus any analyst studying performance from one period or company to another should be aware of the potential for distortion and try to obtain as much information as possible about spending in these areas.

Why are they called discretionary costs and what other examples are there?

Discretionary costs are those which can be varied at the discretion of management, without any impact on the short term operations of the business. Other examples would be training, longer term building maintenance and any money spent on people who work on longer term issues.

Why is the Profit & Loss Account the accounting document which is most commonly seen by managers inside companies?

Because it has proved to be the most practical and effective of the three accounting documents for the internal running of a business. Because of this usefulness, the application of the P & L Account has extended way beyond its original requirement to produce the results of a total company for an accounting year. Now there are half yearly, quarterly, monthly, even weekly P & Ls; they are produced by product, by market segment, by region, even by major customer.

There is more about internal reporting in Chapter 7.

Is this focus on the P & L a good thing?

This focus is generally beneficial because of the information and the insights which it brings to the management of the business. But there is also a danger. The Profit & loss Account only tells part of the story. The Cash Flow and Balance Sheet may be more difficult to produce for shorter periods and for separate units but, as we saw in the first two chapters, they are vitally important. In the case of Cash Flow, the very survival of the business depends upon it.

How does the P & L Account relate to Cash Flow?

It is closely related because it uses many of the same headings but there are substantial differences in the amounts during particular accounting periods. It is possible for a business making profit to be negative on cash and vice versa.

As we will see in Chapter 5, it is possible to produce a Cash Flow Statement in a format which shows clearly the relationship with P & L and illustrates why profit has or has not been generated as cash in a particular period.

How does the P & L Account relate to the Balance Sheet?

They are fundamentally different documents with different purposes. The P & L measures the financial performance of a business over a period, whereas the Balance Sheet is a snapshot of assets, liabilities and sources of funds at the end of that period. They are related because the bottom line of the P & L goes to the Balance Sheet as Retained Profits and, as we saw in Chapter 2, profits must be represented by changes to Net Assets.

Can I now find out more about the Balance Sheet?

Turn to the next chapter.

Reinforcement questions

(1)   What is the correct definition of Sales in a P & L Account?

  (a)   the amount received in cash
  (b)   the orders received
  (c)   the amounts charged for goods delivered

(2) If a company paid rent for year 2 in advance during year 1, in which year's P & L would it show as a cost?

(3) If stock was purchased in year 1 but was sold in year 2, which year's P & L would it appear in?

(4) What is the most frequent breakdown of costs within a P & L Account?

(5) What would be the normal definition of Gross Profit in a manufacturing business?

(6) What would be the normal definition of Gross Profit in a retailing business?

(7) Give three examples of management judgements which might have an impact on the Operating Profit of a company.

(8) What other examples are there of discretionary costs, apart from Research?

(9) Depreciation is always shown in Cost of Sales, true or false?

(10) Depreciation is the only cost which is a book entry, true or false?

4

The Balance Sheet

"You know, we accountants are
a much misunderstood lot"

Sir Kenneth Cork

What does a Balance Sheet tell you about a business?

It tells you a number of things. It tells you where the money has come from to fund the business and the assets which have been bought with that money. It also shows the amount of external liabilities. If the Balance Sheet balances it confirms that all the money put in to the business has been accounted for.

Is the Balance Sheet the most important of the three accounting documents?

In one sense yes, because it is the central control mechanism within which the P & L Account and Cash Flow are contained. This was illustrated by the various transactions in Chapter 2.

In terms of interpretation and interest however, the Balance Sheet has decreased in importance in recent times. Though people in conversation may talk about 'reading a balance sheet' as a generic phrase for interpreting a set of accounts, the Balance Sheet on its own does not always tell you that much about a company. This applies particularly to businesses which do not have many physical assets but are still very successful—for example consultancy and computer software businesses.

Is the "Net Assets equals Shareholders Funds" structure used in Chapter 2 now the standard?

No, there is no worldwide standard. The structure in Chapter 2 is common in the UK but there are other formats. Perhaps the most common alternative is the original traditional layout which shows "Total Assets equals Total Liabilities".

How would the Balance Sheet from Chapter 2 look under that layout?

It would look like this:

ASSETS	equals	LIABILITIES	
Fixed Assets		Share Capital	£10,000
Vehicle	£2,940	Profit & Loss A/C	£490
Total Fixed Assets	£2,940	Shareholders Funds	£10,490
Current Assets		Loans	£2,000
Stock	£1,000		
Debtors	£2,750	Creditors	£1,000
Cash	£6,800		
Total Current Assets	£10,550		
Total Assets	£13,490	Total Liabilities	£13,490

What are the main arguments for this layout?

Some argue that it was the original format of accounting so why change it? Others point to the greater simplicity of having no negatives in either column. In the "Net Assets equals Shareholders Funds" layout, the Creditors and Loans are shown as a reduction of assets and this can be difficult for some people to relate to. Also the level of gearing—Loans in relation to Shareholders Funds—is more easy to see when both are on the Liabilities side.

And the arguments against?

People often find it confusing to think of Shareholders Funds as a liability and it is less easy for shareholders to see the way in which their money has been used, as we were able to show in Chapter 2. But, in the end, it's a matter of personal preference and custom and practice. As long as it is understood that the differences are ones of layout rather than principle, it should not adversely affect interpretation.

How can Shareholders Funds be a liability?

If you see the company as a legal entity, the share capital invested and the profit retained are liabilities of the company to its shareholders. The money is liable to be returned to the shareholders if ever the company is wound up, assuming that there are sufficient funds after the assets have been sold.

To what extent does the Balance Sheet reflect the position throughout the year?

Not necessarily at all. The Balance Sheet shows the position on the last day of the accounting period only. It is often referred to as a "snapshot" and this sums up its limitations well. The merry go round of business, as recorded in the Cash Flow and Profit and Loss Account, is stopped and the Balance Sheet shows the financial position on that one day.

Doesn't this mean that you can easily be misled by using the Balance Sheet to analyse the financial position of a business?

Very much so. Even if management do not go in for deliberate manipulation, there may well be other reasons why the position is not typical of other times of the year. The most obvious factor is the impact of seasonal business patterns in many companies; an analyst looking at the December Balance Sheet of a business with substantial Christmas trade could produce highly misleading ratios of stock and debtor levels.

Even if the business is not seasonal, distortions are possible. For instance, borrowing could have been repaid the day before the year end and the Balance Sheet would not therefore reflect the position of the previous 364 days of the year.

Do you get deliberate manipulation?

Yes, it happens frequently. The term often used is "window-dressing". For instance the decision to repay borrowings the day before the year end might be timed purely to make the company appear less exposed to debt in its Balance Sheet.

So how do analysts cope with this problem?

They have to be careful and enquiring, understanding the seasonal impact and looking for clues to test out whether, deliberately or otherwise, the snapshot distorts the picture. For instance, one clue with regard to borrowing could be the amount of interest in the P & L; this would provide a guide to the average debt throughout the year.

So would the Fixed Assets in the Balance Sheet include those which were bought the day before the period end?

Yes, as well as all which have been bought in the past and are still owned, less accumulated depreciation.

How does depreciation impact the Balance Sheet?

It reduces the Fixed Assets figure in the Balance Sheet as it is applied each year. As shown in Chapter 2, there is a simultaneous reduction to Shareholders' Funds in the Balance Sheet, as this same amount is charged to the P & L.

Who decides the period over which Fixed Assets are depreciated?

This is decided by management amd reviewed for reasonableness by the Auditors. It should reflect the expected life of those assets, as far as can be accurately forecast. As with many issues in accounting, it is a matter of judgement.

What are typical depreciation periods?

Plant and Machinery and Fixtures and Fittings would often be around ten years; computers more like three to five years; cars about the same. It all depends on the company's policy towards asset renewal. If the Fixed Asset is property, the land is not depreciated at all and the buildings will normally be depreciated over forty or fifty years.

To what extent does a Balance Sheet provide accurate valuations of assets?

The Balance Sheet does not and was never intended to value individual assets or the business as a whole. This is because assets are included in the Balance Sheet at the price paid (historic cost) less depreciation, not at their market value. Yet inexperienced analysts often assume that the assets do reflect current values. For instance it would be naïve for a lender to assume that the Balance Sheet valuations provide security for repayment of a loan; even more naive for a potential investor to assume that assets always provide an underpinning to the share price.

If for instance we looked at the assets in the Balance Sheet shown earlier in this chapter and the extent to which the numbers reflect true value, we would need to ask a number of questions, for example:

- Is the vehicle now worth £2,940 after the one month's depreciation? We all know how vehicles lose value as we drive them from the showroom so this vehicle is almost certainly worth less than £2,940.
- Is the stock worth the £1,000 we paid? What if we had to get rid of it in a forced sale?
- Will the debtor pay in full; could there be an invoice dispute or will the customer go bust before the account is settled?

When you think about these questions it becomes clear that there is only one asset where the valuation is clear and undisputed; and that asset is cash. In every other case it depends on the assumption being made and is not a clear or simple issue. Even with cash there are complexities, for example which currency is it in and can it be converted back into the Balance Sheet currency?

Analysts have to understand the Balance Sheet's original and fundamental purpose. This fundamental purpose is to show how the business has been financed and what management have done with the money. The Balance Sheet should not be expected to value assets at any particular time—something that it was never designed to do.

What about assets which appreciate in value, like property for instance?

Though depreciation is accounted for, the normal practice with appreciation is to ignore it, until the property is sold. This is another example of the prudence concept, assuming a likely reduction in value but not an increase.

But aren't there some examples of property and other assets being revalued upwards to market value?

Some companies in some countries have gone against the normal practice and have revalued land and buildings to their market value at the Balance Sheet date. It all depends on what is allowed under the regulatory system in each country. For instance, this practice is not allowed in the USA but is quite common in the UK and some other European countries.

So how does it still balance?

Because there is a double entry in the Balance Sheet. Fixed Assets go up by the amount of the revaluation and there is a new entry in Shareholders Funds of the same amount, termed a Revaluation Reserve.

This represents a theoretical and unrealised profit which is not available for dividend; thus it must be kept separate from normal retained profits in the Balance Sheet. Looking for this entry is a good way of finding out if a revaluation has been carried out.

Why doesn't every company revalue property?

Because it is not in line with normal accounting practice and the Balance Sheet's fundamental purpose. There are more arguments against than for revaluation. The arguments against are as follows:

- It is subjective and dependent on the view of the valuer. Experts are brought in for property valuations of this kind but they can come up with widely differing values.
- In particular a property value depends on the likely use by a buyer, which may be difficult to establish and could be very different from the company's current operations.
- It is transient and will become out of date overnight. Thus there has to be a policy about periodic updating.
- It is expensive; expert valuers have to be paid fees for their services.
- It will make asset values and depreciation higher and the return the management are making on that investment will therefore appear lower.
- It will make comparison between companies even more difficult, unless everyone has revalued at the same time.

Against this has to set the benefits:

- It will make the Balance Sheet appear more secure to a lender
- It can provide support for a faltering share price, where there are good underlying assets
- It gives the Shareholders a better idea of the true value of their assets, and the return which they should be getting.

On balance most accounting and regulatory bodies take the view that, though leaving property at original cost may have some disadvantages, regular revaluation poses too many practical problems to be accepted as normal practice. There is no reason of course why such revaluations cannot be carried out and included in a note to shareholders elsewhere in the Annual Report.

Is stock ever revalued?

The prudence concept determines that stock is not revalued upwards under normal accounting principles as that would be anticipating a profit before it takes place. The same prudence concept also means however that there will, in certain circumstances, need to be a downwards revaluation. This is because the principle for stock valuation is "cost or net realisable value, whichever is the lower". Thus, if stock has declined in value compared to its cost of purchase because of obsolescence or change in circumstances, it will need to be shown at that lower value. This is yet another area where management judgement is required because agreeing that realisable value is rarely an exact science.

How are debtors valued?

Debtors are valued at the amount invoiced to customers, assuming that payment is likely to be received. Again the prudence concept and judgement come into play here; if there is any doubt about all or part of an amount being paid by a customer, an estimate or provision for doubtful debts has to be made. If the customer is unlikely to pay, the whole debt should be written off.

Are intangible assets ever brought into the Balance Sheet?

Yes, though accountants are generally reluctant to show intangibles unless they are sure that there is future value. Examples of intangibles which might appear in a Balance Sheet are magazine titles for a publisher or exploration rights for an oil company. However these can only be included in a Balance Sheet if they have been purchased and have a future value. There also has to be a policy about depreciation, just as there would be for a Fixed Asset.

What about intangibles which have never been bought but have been built up over time, for example brands and trade names?

These will not appear in the Balance Sheet as no transaction has taken place to put them there and it is not easy to obtain an accurate valuation of their future benefit to the business. Also, it is not the role of the Balance Sheet to show all assets and their values; only amounts which have been spent on those assets which have been purchased in the past. There has been pressure for intangible assets such as brands to be shown and valued in Balance Sheets and various methods have been put forward, but this has not received general favour. It would bring in even more subjectivity than the valuation of properties and would be of questionable benefit. As with property, there is nothing to stop the management stating their view on the value of intangibles as a separate note if they want to give shareholders this extra information.

But isn't goodwill shown in Balance Sheets?

It depends on the accounting convention in the country concerned but, generally, yes. This arises when one company takes over another and buys goodwill as part of the deal. Effectively goodwill is the excess of the purchase price of the acquisition, over the fair value of the net assets acquired. For example:

Company A buys company B	100m
Company B's net assets	60m
	____
Goodwill (balancing figure)	40m
	____

This 40m is the premium paid over the fair value of the net assets and represents all the combined reasons why company A is prepared to pay such an excess to buy the company—its brands, its future potential, synergies between the two companies etc. It has to appear in the Balance Sheet of Company A because 100m cash has been taken out and only 60m net assets brought in to replace it. It is also right that it should be shown; shareholders' money has been spent and it should be accounted for.

Does this acquired goodwill stay in the Balance Sheet for ever?

No, it is depreciated rather like a fixed asset, though the term "amortisation" is normally used. Goodwill is amortised over an agreed period to reflect the expected life of the acquired company as a separate business. If the business is likely to have a short life as a separate entity or if it is in a rapidly changing environment, the write off period will be short. Each year the company must be able to satisfy the Auditors that the acquired business has future value, otherwise the goodwill must be written off accordingly.

What other liabilities are there in a Balance Sheet, apart from borrowings and creditors for raw materials as shown in Chapter 2?

There could be creditors for other supplies within Cost of Sales, for example energy costs invoiced but not yet paid, and also amounts owing for expenses, for example advertising charges.

What if the invoice has not yet come in and/or if the amount is uncertain?

This is shown as a liability via the creation of an accrual as mentioned in Chapter 3. Accruals ensure that all such amounts are included as costs in the P & L and as liabilities in the Balance Sheet. If there is a large amount of uncertainty such estimates are often called provisions.

So the only liabilities in a Balance Sheet apart from borrowings, are creditors, accruals and provisions?

Creditors, accruals and provisions are the main liabilities which operating management can control but there may also be other non-operating liabilities, for example tax owing to the government and dividends declared but not yet paid to shareholders. All these would be collected together under the heading of Current Liabilities. There might also be longer term liabilities for items such as pensions and other retirement benefits.

What is the relationship between Shareholders' Funds in the Balance Sheet and a company's value on the Stock Market?

There is no direct relationship. The Shareholders' Funds (or Equity) represents the money which shareholders have put into the business via initial capital investment and via retained profits over time. A company's Stock Market value reflects future expectations and will, for a successful business, normally exceed the Shareholders' Equity figure. In fact the excess over Shareholders' Equity can be seen as the value added by management and is often used by analysts as a measure of success.

What does the Retained Profits figure in the Balance Sheet actually mean?

It is a record of all profits which have been made in the past and have not been distributed to Shareholders. It enables Shareholders to see what they have invested in the business via this route. It is not a cash figure—the assets which have been purchased with the money are shown on the other side of the Balance Sheet.

With all these reservations about the Balance Sheet not valuing assets and not showing current shareholder value, what use is it to analysts?

We stated earlier that it is a document which is of less use to analysts than is often assumed and there is frequently more emphasis on the P & L Account and Cash Flow Statement. However, despite its limitations, the Balance Sheet is a valuable supplement to analysis of the other two documents.

If we think of the three perspectives mentioned in Chapter One—manager, shareholder and banker:

Managers can see the cost of the assets that have been invested in the business and on which they are expected to make a return. The values may not be current but they still represent what has, in the past, been provided for them to use in the business.

Shareholders can see what they have put in and the assets which have been purchased with their money.

Bankers can see the amount of borrowings which have been taken out, and the assets which are available as security. They would need to make further enquiries to know up to date values but at least they have some idea of the assets owned by the company.

Would analysts normally look at two Balance Sheets for different years and compare them?

Yes, and that is another reason why the Balance Sheet provides useful scope for analysis, despite its limitations. Bankers in particular will look for changes in assets from one year to another, to assess the way in which cash has been used. As we will see in the next chapter, it is possible to produce a cash flow statement with changes to assets as a major part of its structure.

Are there standard ways of producing cash flow statements of this kind?

Read on to the next chapter.

Reinforcement questions

(1)   What does it mean if the Balance Sheet fails to balance, assuming that the Net Assets side is lower than Shareholders Funds?

(2)   Which of the two Balance Sheet layouts makes it easier to assess a company's gearing?

(3)   Suggest an example of 'window-dressing', used by a Financial Director who wants to show as much cash as possible in the Balance Sheet.

(4)   Suggest an extreme example of a seasonal business whose results might be distorted by a Balance Sheet at a particular date.

(5)   Would the Balance Sheet value of a piece of plant and machinery, depreciated over ten years, normally be higher or lower than its market value at the end of the first year? At the end of the fifth year? At the end of the tenth year?

(6)   Which asset in the Balance Sheet is most likely to represent its realisable value?

(7)   Which country does not allow upward revaluation of property?

(8)   How can you tell from a Balance Sheet that such a revaluation has taken place?

(9)   What is the principle used to determine stock valuation in the Balance Sheet?

(10)   In what circumstances might brands appear in a Balance Sheet?

(11)   What is the difference between a creditor, an accrual and a provision?

(12)   What is the difference between Share Capital and Shareholder's Equity?

5

The Cash Flow Statement

"Profits can be manufactured by creative accounting but creating cash is impossible"

Terry Smith

What is cash flow?

In some ways it is not an accounting concept at all; it is merely the actual bank account movement of a company during a period. There is a certain amount of money in the bank at the beginning of the period and a certain amount at the end: the cash flow is the change in the bank account during the intervening period.

So does that mean that a Cash Flow Statement just shows cash in and cash out?

The simplest forms of Cash Flow Statement are like that. But a number of other ways have been developed to show cash flow in more meaningful form.

But what could be more meaningful than cash in and cash out?

It is true that this is a simple concept but, for most businesses, it is a long and cumbersome listing. In fact it is the company's bank statement and a bank statement is not a good management information document. You have to have some form of summary and classification.

What is the normal period for which a Cash Flow Statement is produced?

The same as the other two accounting documents. Externally it has to be reported each year, internally it is normal to have monthly or quarterly reports. Also, in view of its importance for survival, there needs to be somebody in the centre managing cash flow day to day, to ensure that enough money is available to meet liabilities as they arise.

Is it always a good thing to have a lot of cash?

Not necessarily, it depends on the future needs of the business. Holding cash which has no obvious purpose is not a good strategy, the money should be invested or returned to shareholders.

So how do you assess whether a Cash Flow Statement shows a good or bad result?

By looking at the cash generated by a business during the period from its operations, not at the amount left at the end.

So what is the normal format of a Cash Flow Statement?

There is no normal format, there are a variety of approaches which we will explore in this chapter. These can be divided into two main methods of presentation. There are no generally accepted labels but, for convenience, we shall call these methods 'Receipts and Payments' and 'Funds Flow'.

The Receipts and Payments method is the approach mentioned above, cash in cash out, rather like a bank statement. This was shown in Chapter 2 as follows (opening cash was zero because this was a business start-up):

Opening Cash	0
Cash in:	
New Share Capital	10,000
Cash received from customers	3,000
New loan	2,000
Total Cash available	15,000
Cash out:	
Vehicle purchase	(3,000)
Stock purchased for cash	(4,500)
Administrator's wages	(500)
Administrative expenses	(200)
Total Cash out	(8,200)
Closing Cash	£6,800

So what does the Cash Flow Statement tell you in this case?

It tells you that the business had £10,000 cash from shares as initial investment but that by the end of the month, this had reduced to £6,800.

By analysing the cash in and the cash out columns, it is possible to find out why.

So why do you need another format when this one is so simple?

Because the other 'Funds Flow' format can make it easier to see what changes have taken place, in particular the relationship between cash flow and profit.

How does that work with the above example?

It is difficult to illustrate with that example as there has only been one accounting period so far. Let's assume that this company has a second month of operating and the cash flow looks like this:

Opening Cash	6,800
Cash in:	
Cash received from customers	20,000
Total Cash available	26,800
Cash out:	
Fixed Asset purchases	(7,000)
Cash paid to suppliers	(19,000)
Administrator's wages	(500)
Administrative expenses	(200)
Total Cash out	(26,700)
Closing Cash	£100

So this company has an adverse cash flow?

Yes, there is an adverse cash flow of £6,700 because the bank account balance has moved from £6,800 to £100.

So why do you need more information?

It is true that the cash flow movement is recorded by this method, but we do not know why it has happened. Is the company losing money or is it merely the consequence of the expansion of a new business?

Won't the Profit & Loss Account tell you this?

Yes, and that's exactly why you need a Profit & Loss Account. But there are ways in which the two documents can be linked together. Let's assume that the Profit & Loss Account for this same period is as follows:

Profit and Loss Account	£	
Sales		22,000
Cost of sales	(17,000)	
Administrator's wages	(500)	
Administrative expenses	(200)	
Depreciation	(200)	
Total costs		(17,900)
Profit		£4,100

So how can we have made a profit when the cash flow was negative?

There are a number of reasons, and the cash flow statement in the 'Funds Flow' format will show you the impact of each. Before we quantify them we can list the possibilities:

- Investment in Fixed Assets, affecting cash flow but not profit
- Cash not yet collected from customers, even though the Sales have been shown in the P & L
- Cash spent on stock, not yet included in the P & L Account

Are there items which work the other way?

Yes. For instance there could be costs of raw materials in the P & L Account which have not yet been paid for in cash.

How do you find out the impact of all these factors?

One way is to look at the opening and closing Balance Sheets of the period, particularly the Stocks, Debtors and Creditors, what is often called Working Capital.

So what is the opening and closing Working Capital of this second period?

The opening figures are the closing figures of period 1, which we saw in the Balance Sheet of Chapter 2. The numbers were:

Stock	1,000
Debtors	2,750
Creditors	(1,000)
Working Capital	£2,750

Why are Creditors a reduction?

Creditors are liabilities, representing money owed to suppliers, thus they reduce the Net Asset position. You are effectively reducing the amount of money you are tying up in Stock and Debtors.

So what are the equivalent figures at the end of the period?

	Opening £	Closing £
Stock	1,000	3,500
Debtors	2,750	4,750
Creditors	(1,000)	(1,500)
Working Capital	£2,750	£6,750

So the increase of Debtors by £2000 means that there is £2000 less in cash flow than there is in the P & L?

Yes, this is confirmed by the fact that Sales were £22,000 whereas cash received was £20,000. And the changes in Stock and Creditors account for the difference between Cost of Sales and cash paid to suppliers.

So how do you bring all this together?

In a Cash Flow Statement that starts with profit and ends with cash flow, showing all the differences along the way.

Where do you start?

By taking the profit of £4,100 and adding back depreciation, ie

Profit	4,100
Depreciation	200
	£4,300

Why do you add back depreciation?

Because this is the first stage in the attempt to arrive at cash flow. Depreciation is an accounting entry which has been taken off to arrive at the profit figure. Since it is not a cash flow, we add it back; effectively we are recalculating the profit figure as it would have been if no depreciation had been charged.

What next?

Now we adjust this figure of £4,300 for the change in Working Capital for the period.

Profit		4,100
Depreciation		200
		4,300
Change in Working Capital		
Increased Stock	(2,500)	
Increased Debtors	(2,000)	
Increased Creditors	500	
		(4,000)
		£300

Couldn't you just have taken the Working Capital change as one number, from 2,750 to 6,750?

You could but this would have given you less information. Now we can see that the negative cash impact is caused partly by the Debtors increase and partly by the Stock increase but this impact has been offset to some extent by the increase in Creditors.

Why is an increase in Creditors a positive cash flow?

Because it is an increase in money owing to suppliers; thus the cash has not yet been paid out.

What does this £300 represent?

It is the cash flow from operating activities, also often called Operating Cash Flow. It is the profit before depreciation, adjusted for the impact of Working Capital. This form of Cash Flow Statement is showing that hardly any of the profit, which is potential cash flow, is coming through as cash because of the impact of the Working Capital increase.

Should Operating Cash Flow always be as high as possible?

In general terms, yes. It would depend on the reason why the cash has been generated; for instance if it had been achieved by cutting discretionary costs too much or by reducing stocks to unrealistic levels, it would not be good for the business. But over the long term, the generation of cash is what creates value for shareholders.

Is this the end of the Cash Flow Statement?

No, because the final answer has to come back to the £6,700 negative cash flow of the period, to explain why this profitable business had £6,800 in the bank at the beginning and £100 at the end.

What else has to be included?

The Fixed Asset purchase. This is a cash flow which is not shown in the P&L Account except by depreciation, which has already been added back.

We thus complete the cash flow statement to arrive at the final cash flow:

Profit		4,100
Depreciation		200
		4,300
Change in Working Capital		
Increased Stock	(2,500)	
Increased Debtors	(2,000)	
Increased Creditors	500	
		(4,000)
		300
Fixed Asset purchase		(7,000)
Net cash flow		£(6,700)

So what does this statement tell you, now that we have finally arrived at the cash flow of £6,700, which we knew already?

It tells you why this profitable business has a negative cash flow, in a much more meaningful way than the original cash in/cash out format. It shows that there are two main causes – an increase in Working Capital and investment in Fixed Assets. It shows the relationship between profit and cash; how and why a profitable business can have a negative cash flow.

Which is more important, this final level of cash flow – (£6,700) – or the Operating Cash Flow – £300 – we worked out earlier?

They are both important and, in the long term, both need to be positive. Operating Cash Flow is more of a short term measure and it would certainly be worrying if it was negative in any one year, unless there were exceptional reasons to justify it.

This final level, often called 'Free Cash Flow' by analysts, can be negative in some years for good and understandable reasons; for instance if there was an unusually high requirement for capital investment. But, in the long term, it must be positive if value is to be created for shareholders.

So there are two routes to cash flow?

Yes, and they both give you the same answer. There is the 'Cash in/Cash out' route which gave us our first figure of negative £6,700. And there is the back door 'Funds Flow' route which arrives at the same number a different way, starting from profit and working back. This second route can be briefly summarised as profit plus depreciation, plus or minus change in Working Capital, minus Fixed Asset investment.

Could there be other entries?

Yes, we have taken a relatively simple example. For instance there could be disposals of Fixed Assets, payments of tax and dividend or issues of new capital.

Which format of Cash Flow Statement is normally seen in published accounts?

The formats have varied widely over the years and there is little standardisation for different countries. Normally it is the 'Funds Flow' format which is shown because this is the most meaningful statement of what is happening in the business, showing the link to profit.

Who looks at Cash Flow Statements?

They tend to be looked at by analysts. They will examine current statements as part of their desire to understand the potential for long term cash generation, which is the key to stock market valuations. They will try to project forward, hoping to ascertain the future cash flows, making allowance for factors which are causing temporary fluctuations

Do they give this more importance than the P&L Account and Balance Sheet?

They look at all three documents and a good analyst will understand the relationships between them. Analysts like cash flow statements because they are not subject to judgement and manipulation like the other accounting statements. Cash at the beginning and cash at the end have to be there to prove the cash flow so there is less scope for manipulation.

Are Cash Flow Statements used both externally and internally?

Yes. The next two chapters will talk more about internal and external reporting

Reinforcement questions

(1) What are the two forms of Cash Flow Statement called?

(2) Why is depreciation added back to profit in a Cash Flow Statement in 'Funds Flow' form?

(3) What will be the impact on cash flow of a reduction in Creditors, adverse or favourable?

(4) What will be the impact on cash flow of a reduction in Debtors, adverse or favourable?

(5)   What will be the impact on cash flow of a reduction in Stock, adverse or favourable?

(6)   Which type of Cash Flow Statement is most normally seen in externally published accounts?

(7)   Why do analysts increasingly look at Cash Flow Statements when analysing company performance?

(8)   What are the main reasons why profit and cash flow will be different?

(9)   What is the difference between Operating Cash Flow and Free Cash Flow?

(10)   What might Shareholders say if a company holds a lot of cash?

6

External reporting

"It is better to be approximately
right than precisely wrong"

Francis Sandilands

What do we mean by external reporting?

Any set of accounts made available publicly to shareholders, and therefore to the outside world.

Are the basic accounting principles – Matching, Prudence, Consistency, Materiality and Going Concern – enough on their own to ensure good external reporting?

No, they provide a foundation and are generally accepted as the underlying principles in all countries and companies that apply recognised business standards. However more regulation is required to guide companies and their auditors about the way specific items should be treated.

Can you give an example of how these basic principles provide the foundation ?

An example would be depreciation. The principle of *matching* confirms that depreciation should be included in the P & L Account, to match the cost of the asset to the results of each year it is held. The principle of *prudence* confirms that, if in doubt, judgement should assume a shorter rather than longer life, thus reducing profits more quickly. The principle of *consistency* confirms that the same method should be used each year, unless there is a fundamental change in policy. The principle of *materiality* confirms that it is not necessary to depreciate small amounts of capital expenditure, for example a few hundred pounds. And the *going concern* principle confirms that you need not take into account the realisable value of the asset unless there are doubts about the future of the company.

Why isn't this enough?

Because you need statements of standard accounting practice to cover the practical issues of interpretation and implementation of these principles.

What kind of issues?

With regard to depreciation, one issue would be the treatment of property as mentioned in Chapter 4; whether you need to depreciate property and whether you would look at land and buildings separately in deciding depreciation levels. Also whether property can be revalued and what rules apply when this happens.

Are these statements of accounting practice international?

Generally no. There has been some work done to establish international standards but there is mixed compliance. Country standards tend to take priority so there are still many differences between practice in different countries.

Why do there have to be differences between countries?

It's a combination of history and differing views about business issues. Agreement is often difficult because there are entrenched views and a reluctance to change to another country's method.

There are also different philosophies in different countries. In Italy, France, Spain and Germany for instance, accounting thinking is mainly tax driven. In the USA, UK, Holland and Australia, it is based more on commercial judgement and business practice.

What would be an example of a major difference between countries?

Perhaps the most fundamental difference has been the treatment of acquired goodwill which was mentioned in Chapter 4. In the UK and some other parts of Europe, the premium paid over asset values for an acquisition used to be written off against past retained profits and not

shown in the Balance Sheet. In the USA however acquired goodwill was taken to the Balance Sheet as an intangible asset and amortised over a number of years. This made UK and USA accounts very difficult to compare.

What's the situation now?

The situation has changed as a result of a UK Accounting Standard in 1998. It is in fact an example of international harmonisation, because the UK has come into line with the USA; acquired goodwill is now shown in the Balance Sheets of UK companies.

What are these statements of accounting practice called?

There are many acronyms used in different countries. In America they call them FAS's – Financial Accounting Standards. Over time the UK Accounting body – the Institute of Chartered Accountants – has gone through a wide range of acronyms – for instance SSAPs, Statements of Standard Accounting Practice, and most recently FRSs, Financial Reporting Standards. The UK body also adds to the confusion by publishing consultative documents at an earlier stage, for example FREDs, Financial Reporting Exposure Drafts, and UITFs, Urgent Issues Task Force reports.

What purpose do these standards serve?

They are really for two purposes; to guide the company as to what is acceptable accounting practice and to provide a framework for the Auditors to protect the shareholders from dubious 'creative' accounting.

What does creative accounting mean?

Choosing the accounting method or making judgments which manipulate the results into what you want them to be, rather than what they would be according to correct accounting principles. A lot of accounting standards are produced to prevent the use of creative accounting.

So do companies have to comply by law?

That depends on the law of each country but generally the answer is no. These statements provide recommended practice but, in most countries, it is possible for a company's management to refuse to comply.

So what's the point then?

Even if there is no force of law behind accounting standards, they provide strong pressure to conform. If a company decides to go against one of the recommended standards, it will need to get the agreement of its Auditors.

What if they don't ask the Auditors, or the Auditors disagree?

In both cases the Auditors are likely to mention the failure to comply in the Auditors Report. For a public company, this could be damaging and could cause a lack of faith in the accounts generally, and a loss of confidence in the company.

What are the main areas of dispute and judgment, where accounting standards are needed?

A lot of them are around complex issues of accounting which are outside the scope of this book, for example, taxation, foreign exchange, pensions, etc. Others are around issues that relate to particular types of business, for instance there is a standard about the accounting treatment of long term contracts, in particular when profits can be taken.

A good example of a standard that was brought in because of concern about creative accounting is the UK SSAP 13, on Research and Development. In the 1970s, Rolls Royce was taking investment in Research to the Balance Sheet and treating it as a Fixed Asset. This increased their profit in the short term and hid the true position from the shareholders. The standard confirms the application of the prudence concept to a particular issue by disallowing this treatment.

Are there other reasons for Accounting Standards?

Yes. Quite a lot of them are about extra disclosure. Public companies are required by Stock Exchange regulations to disclose certain information and accounting standards lay down the detail of how it should be done. For example there are accounting standards on the calculation of Earnings per Share and the detail of segmental reporting.

There are also standards which require disclosure beyond what would normally be required from accounts. For instance, post Balance Sheet events and contingent liabilities such as guarantees of loans for other companies.

What drives the production of new standards?

Concern from Auditors and from shareholder representatives (for example Stock Exchange analysts) that the present accounting methods are not providing a 'true and fair view' of the company's affairs. This 'true and fair' principle underlies much accounting thinking; if present rules are being abused or do not provide good information, an accounting standard is likely to be developed.

Do companies have to declare that they are complying with standards?

No. They have to produce a statement of accounting policies and these will often refer to particular standards and the way they have been interpreted. For example, on depreciation, they might quote the accounting standard on property valuation, state how far they have complied with it and quote the number of years over which assets are being depreciated.

And the Auditors Report?

That would normally only mention accounting standards if there was a failure to comply which they found unacceptable. The signing of an Auditors Report without qualification is, by implication, confirmation that standards have been adhered to.

What do you mean by 'without qualification'?

The qualification of an Auditors report is stating that the accounts do *not* give a true and fair view of the company's affairs, that some problem exists. A report without such qualification gives a clean bill of health.

What are the most obvious examples of Standards which have closed up loopholes?

Leasing is a good example. Companies discovered that leasing deals were a good way of hiding the true extent of a company's borrowing, because leases did not appear on the Balance Sheet. Thus a company could buy a fixed asset, borrow the money from a finance company but ask them to treat it as a lease from a legal point of view. This meant that there was no asset and no liability on the Balance Sheet.

An accounting standard was brought in to differentiate between 'finance leases' and 'operating leases'. Finance leases were those of the type described above and these had to be shown on both sides of the Balance Sheet, as if the assets had been bought with borrowed money. Only 'operating leases' – those that involve more than a financial transaction – could be kept 'off Balance Sheet'

This standard is an example of another important accounting principle "substance over form". It is the commercial reality of the transaction rather than its legal status which should drive the accounting method.

Is it possible for accounting standards to stop all creative accounting?

No, there are always areas which require management judgement and accounting standards can only provide a framework within which to make that judgment. For instance there are accounting standards on stock valuation and the general principle, as mentioned in Chapter 4, is that stock should be valued at cost or realisable value, whichever is the lower. With regard to debtors, the principle is that there has to be a reasonable provision for 'doubtful' debts.

In the end however, someone has to make a judgement about what is a good estimate of the realisable value of obsolete stock, just as someone has to make a judgement about what represents a 'doubtful' debtor. Accounting standards do not help here; all the Auditors can do is question the assumptions and make an assessment of their validity. In practice, it may not be too difficult to be 'creative' if management is determined to mislead its shareholders in the short term.

Do accounting standards determine the layout of the accounting documents?

Yes, together with legislation, they do and it is here that there are many variations over time and between countries. Cash Flow Statements in particular have had many formats over the years as reporting practice and new disclosure requirements have evolved. Sometimes this leads to documents becoming over complex, for example the P & L has become more difficult to interpret because of an accounting standard which requires the results of ongoing businesses to be separated from those which have been sold. This was well intentioned but perhaps counter productive because of the complexity it creates in some businesses.

Do companies have to comply with accounting standards when it comes to internal reporting?

No, but there are many other factors to consider. These are covered in the next and final chapter.

Reinforcement questions

(1) What are the five basic accounting concepts which provide a foundation for accounting practice?

(2) Which has the most authority, a FRED or a FRS?

(3) Is a qualified Auditors Report a good thing?

(4) What would be the likely impact on the share price of a major company, if it received a qualified Auditors Report?

(5) What is the difference between a Finance and an Operating Lease?

(6) What impact does the accounting standard on leases have upon the reported gearing of the company?

(7) Why are debtors such an important judgement area for accounting in many businesses?

7

Internal reporting

"Money is as much a reality as
the Blessed Trinity"

Monsignor Ralph Brown

Are all three financial statements used for internal management of the business?

Yes, because any information required to be published externally for shareholders must also be important for the directors and managers of the business. They will be held accountable so they need to fully understand the statements and the reasons for the numbers which they show.

They also need to assess management performance through the Profit & Loss Account, to control assets through the Balance Sheet and to understand, via the Cash Flow Statement, how cash moves in and out of the business. The three financial statements are the central framework for control of the business and management ignore them at their peril.

I can understand that at a corporate level, but what about within the divisions or business units; are the three statements produced for these?

This depends on the extent of autonomy allowed to divisions. Generally the more the autonomy, the more likely the division is to have all three statements as part of its management reporting structure. Those companies who do not allow much autonomy and have a centralised approach to management, may decide that it is only necessary or feasible to have a Profit & Loss Account.

But shouldn't all business units be responsible for cash flow and control of assets?

In principle yes but it is a matter of management judgement how far this is reflected in financial reports. For instance, someone managing a brand or a group of products may best be managed through P & L only, because it is not practical to allocate centralised assets which are shared with other parts of the business.

Does this mean that managers are not motivated to control cash and manage assets?

Unfortunately yes. It is one of the weaknesses of many internal management accounting systems. There is however no point in trying to develop separate financial statements unless they are meaningful and motivating to managers. One answer is to develop other ways of making managers accountable for the decisions they make which impact cash and assets. This can be done by developing performance measures to support the P & L: for instance, Stock and Debtor ratios.

Do internal accounts use the same accounting concepts as external ones?

Usually but not necessarily. Some companies keep the two closely aligned throughout their reporting. Others say that there are separate objectives so why should internal accounts use the same principles? In other words they see a clear distinction between:

—Financial accounts for external publication
—Management accounts for internal use

Well known examples are Unilever and the Phillips organisation which have used the replacement cost concept to value assets internally but follow the normal historical cost basis for published accounts.

Is this a good idea?

This is another question of management judgement. Phillips and Unilever would argue that they need not be restricted to conventional accounting when making decisions internally; that replacement cost is a better way of valuing assets for a number of management purposes.

Others would say that this can get too complicated and that it is better and simpler to stick to external principles whatever their limitations.

Are budgets and financial plans produced in the same format, using the three accounting documents as a framework?

Generally, yes, because one of the purposes of a forward plan is to compare with actuals, thus the same terminology and financial reports should be used.

What about terminology, is this the same as for external accounts?

Not necessarily. Very few companies stick totally to the standard terms for internal purposes and there are enormous differences. Often companies will use their own unique internal language.

Where are the biggest differences?

It happens in all three financial statements but it is the P & L which has perhaps the most variations. Though the 'Sales less Cost' equation applies throughout, there are many variations in cost classification and in profitability levels.

So at least Sales are consistently reported?

Again, not necessarily. Internally there may be more information, perhaps including sales before and after VAT, perhaps showing discounts separately. Internally there is a tendency to want more detail, to encourage investigation and discussion.

Isn't the 'Sales less Cost of Sales equals Gross Profit' format used universally?

No. It is perhaps the most common structure used externally and internally but there are many variations. Even if the Gross Profit structure is used, there is no guarantee that the term is defined exactly the same way between companies.

Why don't they all use the same terms?

It's partly a question of history. Companies have evolved in their separate ways and see no benefit in changing to suit some standard; they may have to change for external reporting but why do so internally?

There is also the question of usefulness for decision making. Gross Profit may not be the most helpful way of categorising costs for this purpose. For instance many companies find that separating variable costs—those that move directly with volume—is a more helpful structure for many types of decisions. Thus their preferred structure may be:

Sales less Variable Costs equals Variable Profit (also often called 'Contribution')

The preferred structure for decision making will vary for different types of business—for instance variable costs may be larger in some companies than others—so it would be wrong to expect all Profit & Loss Accounts to be the same for internal management and control.

What about expenses? Is the breakdown between Selling, Distribution and Administration which was described in chapter 3 a universal one?

No, there are many different ways of splitting costs and the 'Selling, Distribution, Administration' (SAD) split is common but by no means universal. Most companies will have varied ways of splitting costs within their accounting systems. For instance there would be a functional split like SAD to show the cost of functions and hold management accountable for cost control, but also a split by cost type (wages, depreciation, rent etc) for the directors to understand and control overall cost structure.

Cost analysis should be driven by the needs of the reports required to run the business, not by any general standard.

Do you always need the full P & L for internal reporting purposes?

No, it depends on the level of the person receiving the report, and their responsibilities. Clearly the Board of Directors will need to see the whole P & L because they are accountable for total performance to the shareholders. But at lower levels, it may be appropriate only to go down to Operating Profit, because the managers concerned are not responsible for Interest, Tax or Dividend.

Could a report for a manager only go down as far as Gross Profit?

Certainly, if that was the extent of the manager's responsibilities and it was not necessary to show him/her the fuller picture. And whether to show someone the full picture is a management rather than a financial judgement; thus there can be no absolute rights or wrongs when it comes to P & L formats. Some companies will create new definitions of profit for internal purposes; for instance the profit after costs controlled by that manager. Thus a P & L for a marketing person might be structured;

	£
Sales	1,000
Cost of Sales	(550)
	———
Gross Profit	450
Controllable costs	(100)
	———
Contribution	£350
	———

The controllable costs would be the marketing costs controlled by this manager but excluding general overheads. The term 'contribution' is a generic phrase used to describe this kind of profit level, after either variable or controllable costs. In some companies there are numerous, cascading levels of contribution, for different decision making purposes and levels of accountability.

What about the Balance Sheet, how is this presented for internal reporting purposes?

Again it varies enormously between companies. At Board level it would probably follow the general format shown in Chapters 2 and 4, because that is what the shareholders see and what the Directors have to understand. The extent to which the Balance Sheet is cascaded down and the format that is used is dependent on a number of factors.

If the responsibility for raising finance—for example the taking out of new loans—is retained at the centre , there is not much point in making management in the operating units accountable for a full Balance Sheet. Thus it may be decided to show only the Assets side of each unit's Balance Sheet to the managers running those divisions—the operational assets for which they are responsible.

But what if these assets are shared with other operating units, for example a factory making products for a number of divisions?

It is precisely these circumstances which cause management to question whether it is worthwhile cascading Balance Sheet reporting down to operating units, particularly in businesses which have a high level of centralisation and integration. The P & L Account may be the only practical reporting tool for day to day management. There may however be a case for the creation of estimated Balance Sheets, for the purpose of evaluating longer term viability of operating units.

But surely wouldn't that involve lots of estimates and allocations?

Yes, but for strategic purposes that is acceptable and necessary, otherwise you would never know the longer term return you are making on the assets invested in the business.

What about cash flow, how is that reported internally, which of the two formats is used?

The 'Funds Flow' format is the most common because, as explained in Chapter 5, it is the most meaningful from a management point of view. The 'Receipts and Payments' format would be less helpful because it would not show the relationship between profit and cash, nor would it show the impact of decisions on cash so concisely.

So does every operating unit have its own Cash Flow Statement in most companies?

Unfortunately no. The same problems apply as with the Balance Sheet. In fact, if you do not have a separate Balance Sheet, most of the entries in a 'Funds Flow' cash statement are not possible, eg Stock, Debtor, Creditor movements. This problem, and the difficulties of solving it, is the main reason why there is too little awareness of cash flow among managers of large and decentralised businesses.

Do you just have to accept this?

No, you try to focus on some key performance indicators which drive cash flow, for instance control of particular elements of Working Capital and Capital Expenditure.

Is this all I need to know about financial reporting?

It is the sort of subject about which there are so many aspects and potential complexities that you could almost go on for ever. We have tried to restrict this briefing to the things which are essential for managers who receive financial statements to understand.

You mean that we have really finished?

Yes, that's it folks.

92

Reinforcement questions

(1) If a division of a big company was relatively autonomous, would it be more or less likely to have a Balance Sheet as part of its reporting structure?

(2) Which concept of cost is used by Phillips and Unilever, as part of their internal reporting?

(3) What are the advantages of using the variable cost/variable profit structure for internal P & Ls?

(4) Which side of the Balance Sheet will be more important for managers in control of a division with no responsibility for raising funds?

(5) Which of the two cash flow formats—'Receipts and Payments' or 'Funds Flow' is more normally used for internal reporting?